IMMORTAL DNA

Kirk Anthony Ford
Immortal DNA

Published by Spines
ISBN: 979-8-89569-240-0

IMMORTAL DNA

KIRK ANTHONY FORD

INTRODUCTION

In the shadowed valleys of human frailty, a profound disquiet stirs—the palpable sense of an unfulfilled promise, a kinship with an eternity left languishing in the mortal coil. This is the enigma that 'Immortal DNA' dares to unravel: the latent power of Sonship, a generational mantle, eluding the grasp of a world in desperate need. Picture, if you will, a society teetering on the brink, where fear and decay hold sway, and the luminous threads of faith lie forgotten, buried under the detritus of ceaseless striving. Can you see it? Can you feel the tremor of change as the earth itself groans, yearning for the emergence of the Sons of God, those fore-ordained to wield the Elijah-Moses mantle? A journey awaits—a climb up the ethereal rungs of Jacob's Ladder, where the Transfiguration is not mere history but a beacon, illuminating the path to life and immortality. But beware, for the ascent is steep, and the secrets of faith are jealously guarded. Are you ready to be awakened?

In every generation, the mantle awaits, whispering through the annals of scripture, a testament to the immortal work of Christ, the prodigy of humanity. Yet, this sacred calling, this invitation to Sonship, remains elusive to so many. Why? It is a question that haunts the corridors of churches and the silent prayers of the devout. The answer, as profound as it is simple, demands a journey through the processes of life and immortality—a journey of faith and manifestation.

Consider the plight of our world, a tapestry frayed by the relentless passage of time, where the darkness of uncertainty casts long shadows upon the human spirit. Fear, like a voracious specter, devours hope, and the promise of salvation seems a distant dream. But what if that promise was closer than we dared to imagine? What if the key to our liberation was already woven into the very fabric of our being?

Allow me to share a story—a narrative not of fiction, but of palpable truth. There was once a man who, much like the rest of us, sought understanding amidst the chaos of life. He searched for years, delving into the scriptures, yearning for a glimpse of the divine blueprint. And then, in a moment of transcendent clarity, he encountered the reality of Sonship. Life, viewed through this new lens, changed irrevocably. This man's transformation is not an isolated tale; it is a beacon, illuminating the path for us all.

The stakes are nothing less than the redemption of humanity itself. If we fail to grasp the mantle, if we falter in our pursuit of Sonship, the world remains shackled to an existence devoid of true purpose. We stand at the precipice of an epoch, where the choice to ascend or to remain is laid bare before us. To embrace our calling is to offer hope to a world bereft of light.

In the chapters that follow, we will embark on an odyssey that transcends time and space. We will explore the significance of the Mount of Transfiguration, not as a distant event, but as a living reality, pulsating with promise for this generation. You will witness the birthing of the current generational mantle through Sonship and understand the intricate processes that govern the dance between mortality and eternity. As the world awaits, its breath held in silent anticipation, a company of Sons will arise, heralds of salvation through Christ.

But how does one navigate the labyrinth of divine mystery? How does one climb the unseen rungs of Jacob's Ladder? Fear not, for this book is not merely a guide but a companion for the journey. It is a vessel of knowledge, brimming with revelations that have been spoken and mentioned throughout the Bible, now unveiled for such a time as this.

As a Summa Cum Laude graduate, a highly decorated Air Force Veteran, a lifetime minister of the gospel, called audibly to Sonship, an eye-witness of Jesus Christ, and an entrepreneur, I, Kirk Anthony, offer you not just words, but a testament of lived experience. The insights contained herein are not just academic exercises but the fruits of a life devoted to seeking and embodying the divine.

So, I invite you, dear reader, to step beyond the veil of the temporal. Join me in the sacred quest for the Immortal DNA that courses through the spiritual lineage of every believer. Let us discover together the power of faith actualized, the manifestation of the divine within us, and the awakening of the Sons of God. The journey ahead is arduous, yet it promises a reward beyond measure—the transformation not only of the innermost man but of the very world around us. Are you ready to begin?

1

———

THE TRANSFIGURATION AND THE ELIJAH-MOSES MANTLE

The Summit of Change

In a time of great tumult and rapid progression, humanity has found itself at the cusp of a revolution both scientific and spiritual. The pages of history are rich with pivotal moments where the trajectory of human existence was altered, but none quite like the transformative event of the Mount Transfiguration. This was more than a mere point in time; it was a nexus of change, a summit where the concept of immortality and Sonship were irrevocably intertwined.

To understand the full gravity of this event, we must traverse the annals of history, to a period where the ancient and the divine intersected in the most extraordinary of ways. The prophets of old spoke of a time when the very essence of life could be altered, when mortality would lose its sting, and the immortal nature of mankind would be revealed.

Centuries passed as these prophecies lay dormant, enshrined within sacred texts, their truths veiled to the eyes of many. Great empires rose and fell, each leaving their indelible mark upon the world, yet none could unlock the secrets of eternal life. Philosophers pondered the nature of existence, and alchemists sought the elusive elixir of life, but the answers remained just beyond reach.

Fast forward to the present, where the quest for longevity has taken on new forms. The scientific community relentlessly pursues genetic breakthroughs, while spiritual seekers delve into ancient wisdom, each searching for the key to transcendence. But what if the answers we seek have been with us all along, encoded within the very fiber of our being?

Why does history matter now, in an age where technology and faith collide with increasing intensity? Because understanding our past is the key to unlocking our future. It is in the reflection of history's mirror that we come to see our true selves, and the potential that lies within.

As we stand at this precipice, looking out into the great expanse of possibility, we must ask ourselves: Are we prepared to embrace the mantle of Sonship? To bear the responsibility of carrying forward the legacy of those who have come before us?

The Mount Transfiguration was more than just a historical event; it was a demonstration of what is possible when the divine touches the mortal. It serves as a beacon of hope, signaling that the path to immortality is not shrouded in mystery, but illuminated by the light of understanding.

The story we now embark upon is not one of fiction, but a tale of transformation that transcends the bounds of time. It is a narrative that weaves together the threads of history, science, and spirituality, crafting a tapestry of truth that speaks to the very soul of humanity.

This is the journey that "Immortal DNA" invites you to join —a voyage into the heart of what it means to be truly alive. As we delve into the depths of this profound topic, we shall uncover the processes that have shaped our understanding of life and immortality. We will explore the significance of the Mount Transfiguration not as a relic of the past, but as a living testament to the power of faith in the present.

In the coming chapters, you will not only learn about the historical milestones that have led us to this point but also come to understand the importance of this knowledge in addressing the challenges we face today. For in the unraveling of this divine mystery, we find the keys to our own evolution, the blueprint for a future where death is but a distant memory.

As you journey through the pages of this book, remember the significance of the Mount Transfiguration, and the promise it holds. It is more than a summit of change; it is a call to arms, an invitation to step into the fullness of our potential as children of the Most High.

The path ahead is steeped in revelation and fraught with challenges, but fear not. For just as the ancients who dared to dream of a world beyond death, we too shall rise to meet the call of destiny. The mantle of Sonship awaits, and with it, the chance to rewrite the story of humanity.

Let us begin.

Elijah and Moses: Bearers of the Mantle

The narrative of immortality is as ancient as the hills that bore witness to the earliest humans, their eyes fixed on the heavens, pondering the stars and their own mortality. It is in this cradle of civilization that our journey into the lives and legacies of Elijah and Moses begins, two colossal figures whose existence and deeds have been etched into the bedrock of biblical history.

From the outset, these characters were set apart. Elijah, a prophet whose very name means "Yahweh is my God," emerged during a time of profound apostasy in Israel, brandishing the power of the word against the idolatry of his day. Moses, the liberator of Israel, was equally distinguished, serving as the conduit through which the laws of God were delivered to a fledgling nation.

Their origins, although shrouded in the mists of antiquity, are pivotal to our understanding. Moses was rescued from the Nile's embrace and raised in the courts of Egypt, only to flee to Midian after an impulsive act of violence. This exile would serve as the crucible for his calling. Meanwhile, Elijah's origins are less clear, with the Scriptures introducing him as a Tishbite of the inhabitants of Gilead, a man who appears almost ex nihilo to challenge the status quo.

As their stories unfold, major milestones mark their paths. Moses' life is punctuated by the burning bush encounter, the Ten Plagues, the parting of the Red Sea, and the delivery of the Ten Commandments. His journey culminates with a vision of the Promised Land, a land he is destined never to enter. Elijah's narrative arc crescendos with his challenge to the prophets of Baal on Mount Carmel, his flight into the wilderness, and his poignant encounter with God in the "still small voice."

Imagine, if you will, the stark contrasts and vivid scenes that these events evoke: the fire that does not consume, the water that stands as a wall, and the quiet whisper that follows the tumult. These are not merely historical footnotes; they are the brushstrokes of divinity upon the canvas of time.

Despite the differences in their stories, both men share a unique distinction. Elijah is taken up into heaven in a whirlwind, an event depicted in art across the ages, his mantle falling to his successor, Elisha. Moses, though his tomb is unknown, is said to have been buried by God Himself, and Jewish tradition holds that he ascended to heaven. These endings are not just extraordinary; they prefigure the mantle of immortality.

Turning to cultural or regional variations, we find that the roles of Elijah and Moses diverge and converge in fascinating ways. In Judaism, Elijah is expected to return as the forerunner of the Messiah, while Moses is revered as the greatest prophet, the lawgiver. In Christianity, both are seen as precursors to Jesus, with their appearance at the Transfiguration linking them directly to the narrative of redemption and eternal life.

What of modern interpretations or adaptations? Today, these figures are often revisited in the context of spiritual leadership, ethical standards, and eschatological expectations. Their lives and legacies continue to inspire art, literature, and film, serving as archetypes of faithfulness amid adversity.

Yet, the journey through their lives is not without its challenges or controversies. Scholars and theologians debate the historicity of the accounts, the nature of their experiences, and the implications of their purported immortality. These debates turn on pivotal questions: Were these men truly touched by the divine, or are their stories allegorical? What can we glean from their experiences that are relevant to our understanding of life and death?

In pondering these questions, we engage in a conversation that transcends the mere academic. We venture into the realm of belief and the heart of what it means to seek something beyond our mortal coil. Is it not the quest for meaning that drives us to explore these ancient tales?

As our exploration draws to a close, consider this: The legacies of Elijah and Moses are not fossilized relics meant to be admired from a distance. They are living testaments to the quest for immortality, to the hope that there is more to this life than the dust from which we came.

In the silence of contemplation, one may almost hear the whisper of the divine, beckoning us to take up the mantle they left behind. Are we ready to answer that call? To walk in their footsteps, in search of physical immortality, and to embody the eternal principles they championed?

The story of Elijah and Moses is far from over. It is a narrative that we continue to write with each act of courage, each moment of faith, and each step we take toward the unknown. Their mantle, the mantle of immortality, awaits all who dare to believe in the possibility of a life beyond the veil of death.

In the pages that follow, may you find not only the echoes of the past but the whispers of a future where the immortal DNA within us all finds its fullest expression. Moses and Elijah, bearers of the mantle, invite us to look beyond the horizon of our understanding and embrace the mystery that is both ancient and ever-new.

The Inheritance of Sonship

In the great tapestry of Christian theology, there exists a thread that weaves through the fabric of belief, one that is both ancient and vibrant. This thread is the concept of Sonship, a principle that stands as a cornerstone within the faith, bridging the temporal with the eternal. It is a term familiar to many, yet its depths are often left unexplored, its riches unclaimed.

Sonship, in its simplest definition, refers to the state of being a son or daughter. Within Christianity, however, it assumes a profound spiritual connotation: it is the bestowed identity of believers as children of God through their faith in Jesus Christ. To be a "son" or "child" of God is to be an inheritor of divine promises and a participant in the divine nature (2 Peter 1:4).

To elaborate, this key element of Sonship encompasses several integral aspects. It implies a relationship built on intimacy and love, much like that between a parent and child. It suggests an inheritance, as a child is traditionally an heir to the parent's legacy. It also denotes a transformation, where the individual is renewed in character to resemble the divine, a process often termed "sanctification."

Tracing the concept's etymology, "Sonship" comes from the Old English "sunnus," akin to the German "Sohn" and the Dutch "zoon," denoting a male child. In the Greek New Testament, the term "υἱοθεσία" (huiothesia) is used, which means "adoption as sons," signifying not just a natural relationship but a legal and spiritual one, conferred upon believers (Romans 8:15).

When contextualized within the broader framework of Christian thought, Sonship transcends mere familial ties, encapsulating the idea of believers being part of the "body of Christ" (1 Corinthians 12:27). It is an inheritance that carries with it the mantle of immortality, a theme that resonates with the accounts of Elijah and Moses, who both experienced a taste of the eternal.

The real-world applications of this concept are manifold. For the individual believer, it is a source of comfort and identity, reassuring them of their place in God's family. For the community, it fosters unity and purpose, as all members are seen as equal heirs to the kingdom of God. In societal terms, it motivates acts of justice and compassion, for if all are God's children, then all deserve to be treated with dignity and love.

However, common misconceptions about Sonship abound. Some may view it as an entitlement to temporal power or material gain, mistaking the inheritance for earthly wealth rather than spiritual riches. Others might see it as an exclusive claim, forgetting that the offer of becoming God's children is open to all who would receive it (John 1:12).

Now, as we wend our way deeper into the intricacies of this divine inheritance, might one ask: How does the mantle of immortality tie into this concept of Sonship? Do we, as modern believers, grasp the full weight of what it means to be heirs of such a legacy?

Consider the lilies of the field, arrayed in splendor, destined to fade. Yet, are we not promised a glory that outshines them, a life that does not succumb to the wilt of time? Indeed, the mantle we inherit is not one of perishable threads, but of eternal fabric, woven by the hand of the Almighty.

It is, therefore, with profound reverence that we must approach this inheritance. For in it lies not only the promise of life everlasting but the calling to live out our earthly days in the light of that undying hope. The mantle we bear is not just for the age to come; it is a present reality that should shape our every thought, word, and deed.

To embody this truth is no small task. It requires a heart willing to yield, a spirit eager to grow, and a life devoted to reflecting the divine. It is a journey marked by trials, yes, but also by triumphs—moments where the immortal within us resonates with the eternal around us.

Let us, therefore, cast off the shackles of temporal concerns and embrace the Sonship that beckons us. For in so doing, we step into a lineage that traces back to the dawn of creation, a family whose legacy is love, whose inheritance is righteousness, and whose destiny is immortality.

As we continue to pen the chapters of our individual stories, let us not forget the grand narrative we are a part of—the inheritance of Sonship that offers us a glimpse of the immortal DNA that resides in each of us, calling us to a life that transcends the boundaries of time and space.

And so, dear reader, as you turn the pages of this volume, may you find not only a theological treatise but also an invitation. An invitation to discover the depth of your divine heritage, to don the mantle of immortality, and to live out the reality of Sonship in a world that yearns for the eternal touch of the Father's love.

2

———

JACOB'S LADDER: THE DNA OF DIVINITY

The Vision of the Ladder

In the stillness of the ancient world, when the earth was draped in the celestial shroud of night, a solitary figure lay asleep upon the rocky terrain. Jacob, the traveler, found repose in a place that was about to become etched into the annals of history. This unassuming patch of earth under the vast expanse of the cosmos would be the backdrop for a revelation that transcends time, a vision that would forever alter the fabric of faith and human understanding. It is here, in the heart of the narrative, where we begin our exploration of the enigmatic spectacle known as Jacob's Ladder.

The story, as chronicled in the sacred texts, unfolds with Jacob en route to find a wife among his kin, stopping to rest at what would later be called Bethel. As slumber took him, he dreamt of a ladder set upon the earth, its top reaching to the heavens, with angels ascending and descending upon it. Above it stood the Lord, who promised the land to Jacob and his offspring, declaring that through his lineage, all the families of the earth would be blessed. Upon waking, Jacob anointed the stone he had used as a pillow, setting it up as a pillar and vowing a tithe to God if He would remain with him on his journey.

To grasp the gravity of this vision, one must delve into the symbolism that permeates its every aspect. The ladder, bridging the gap between heaven and earth, represents the connection between the divine and the mortal, an axis mundi where communication and interaction between realms are possible. The ascending and descending angels denote a continuous exchange, perhaps the flow of divine will and human aspiration.

Consider, for a moment, the implications of such a vision. What does it signify for a man to witness heavenly beings traversing to and from the earth? Could it be a testament to an intimate relationship between Creator and creation, an assurance of guidance and guardianship?

Some interpretations suggest that the ladder symbolizes the path to enlightenment or spiritual ascent, with each rung representing a step towards a higher state of being. Others see it as a metaphor for the fluctuating fortunes of Jacob's own descendants, the Israelites, who would experience both exalted triumphs and devastating tribulations.

With a tapestry of interpretations, it is crucial to examine the historical context and analyze how this vision has been perceived over the centuries. Scholars and theologians have dissected the narrative, bringing forth insights grounded in cultural, religious, and esoteric schools of thought. Each perspective sheds light on different facets of the vision, contributing to a mosaic of meanings that enrich our understanding.

Moreover, the tangible elements of this event bear significance. The stone, for instance, is not merely a geological feature but a consecrated monument marking a holy encounter. Jacob's anointing of the stone with oil transforms it into a Bethel, a 'House of God', a physical testament to the sacred experience.

One could question the literal nature of this vision. Was the ladder a dream-inspired metaphor, a divine message coded in the subconscious imagery of a weary traveler? Or, could it be a literal experience, an actual glimpse into the celestial workings beyond our mortal comprehension?

To elucidate complex terms within the narrative, let's consider the original language. The Hebrew word 'sulam', translated as 'ladder', could also be rendered as 'staircase' or 'ramp', broadening our visual interpretation. Similarly, the term 'mal'akhim', meaning 'angels', also translates to 'messengers', suggesting a broader role than merely spiritual beings.

Now, let's pause to reflect on the significance of the promise made at the ladder's peak. Does not this covenant echo through the ages, influencing the course of entire nations? How often do we see the ripples of ancient promises in the sands of modernity?

In conclusion, the vision of the ladder stands as a multifaceted jewel in the crown of biblical narratives. Its symbolic richness offers a wellspring of spiritual insight, philosophical contemplation, and theological discourse. As we draw our gaze from the celestial spectacle that Jacob beheld, we are left with the enduring image of a bridge between heaven and earth, a promise of presence and protection, and a legacy that would shape the destiny of countless generations. The ladder, set firmly on the earth with its apex piercing the heavens, remains an eternal emblem of hope, connection, and divine providence.

DNA as the Ladder of Life

In the intricate dance of life, where the tangible meets the immortal, the double helix of DNA spirals like a ladder, echoing the biblical Jacob's Ladder in form and function. It is a structure fundamental to the very essence of life, bearing the code that scripts our existence. As we delve deeper into the scientific revelations and spiritual manifestation of these two ladders, we find ourselves on the precipice of understanding the blueprint for eternal life.

Like the rungs of a celestial ladder, the sequences of nucleotides in DNA bridge the gap between generations, carrying the whispers of our ancestry into the future. The significance of DNA in the scientific world is akin to the importance of Jacob's Ladder in the spiritual realm; both serve as conduits for transcendence, Transfiguration, and transformation. The purpose of this exploration is to unravel the parallels between these two, seemingly divergent, concepts and to grasp the insights they offer in the quest for immortality. However, one must remember that this entire quest is led by faith in the hope of glory!

The criteria for comparison emerge from their foundational roles: both DNA and Jacob's Ladder are seen as pathways—biological and spiritual, respectively. DNA is the biological staircase that allows traits to ascend or descend the generations, while Jacob's Ladder is the spiritual staircase that bridges the earthly and the divine.

Direct comparison reveals that both subjects share a symbolic similarity in their depiction of connectivity. DNA connects cells, individuals, and species, threading the needle of life through the fabric of time. Jacob's Ladder, in its biblical context, connects the physical to the spiritual, man to God, earth to heaven. Each step on the ladder, each twist in the helix, is a testament to the continuum of existence.

In direct contrast, however, the DNA helix is a tangible reality, a structure that can be observed and manipulated through science. Jacob's Ladder, on the other hand, remains within the ethereal dimensions of faith and symbolism. One is a physical entity, the other a spiritual concept; one is studied through microscopes and sequencers, the other through scripture and meditation.

Visual aids, like diagrams of the DNA molecule and artistic renditions of Jacob's Ladder, can serve to highlight these concepts. The twisting ladder of DNA, paired with the envisioned ladder reaching to the heavens, provides a stark illustration of the harmony between the corporeal and the spiritual.

Analysis and insights gleaned from these comparisons suggest that both DNA and Jacob's Ladder are not merely static entities but dynamic pathways. They offer a means of ascent and descent—be it the flow of genetic information or the exchange between higher and lower states of being. They hint at the possibility of evolution, both physical and spiritual, and the potential for reaching an ultimate state.

In contemporary relevance, the quest for eternal life is more than a spiritual longing; it is a scientific endeavor. Advancements in genetic engineering and biotechnology echo the dream of transcending mortal limitations, much like the aspirational symbolism of Jacob's Ladder. Both narratives, one rooted in ancient text and the other in modern science, reflect humanity's enduring pursuit of the eternal, the perfect, and the divine.

As we continue to explore the depths of these parallels, the questions emerge: Can we unlock the secrets of our DNA to find the key to immortality as prophesied by spiritual wisdom? Is the ladder within us, encoded in our very cells, awaiting the day when we can ascend to a new realm of existence?

The notion that our biological makeup contains the potential for everlasting life is not just a scientific hypothesis; it resonates with the age-old human desire for connection with the eternal. The idea that we carry within us a ladder to transcendence—like the angels traversing Jacob's dream—invites us to contemplate our place in the universe and our ultimate destiny.

Indeed, the ladder of life, whether viewed through the lens of faith or the microscope of science, beckons us to climb. It stands as a symbol of hope, a challenge to our understanding, and a bridge to the infinite. As we scale the rungs of knowledge and faith, we may find that the journey itself is as vital as the destination, and that perhaps, in the grand design of existence, we are all, in our essence, immortal.

In conclusion, DNA and Jacob's Ladder, as complex as they are profound, are not merely strands of life or the steps of a dream. They are the very scaffolding upon which we build our understanding of existence and the pursuit of the everlasting. As we turn the page on this chapter, we carry with us the image of life's ladder, twining skyward, inviting us to ascend to the heights of our potential.

Connecting the Divine and the Earthly

"There are also celestial bodies, and bodies terrestrial: but the glory of the celestial is one, and the glory of the terrestrial is another. There is one glory of the sun, and another glory of the moon, and another glory of the stars: for one star differeth from another star in glory. So also is the resurrection of the dead. It is sown in corruption; it is raised in incorruption: It is sown in dishonor; it is raised in glory: it is sown in weakness; it is raised in power: It is sown a natural body; it is raised a spiritual body. There is a natural body, and there is a spiritual body. (1 Corinthians 15:40-44)."

In a world where the corporeal dances with the ethereal, the quest for a bridge between the two realms has been a perennial pursuit. At the heart of this quest lies a significant issue that strikes at the core of human existence: the seeming chasm that separates the spiritual from the physical. It is an age-old dichotomy that has manifested in countless philosophies and religions, each seeking to reconcile the material with the spiritual.

The crux of the problem lies in our intrinsic yearning for a connection with something greater than ourselves, coupled with the limitations of our mortal coil. This yearning has driven us to seek out metaphors and models that might illuminate a path toward unification. It is a challenge that demands resolution, for without a bridge to connect these two realms, we are left grappling in the dark, unable to fully grasp our place in the cosmos or to harness the full potential of our existence. (Reference "Immortal Mentor").

Left unaddressed, this divide can lead to a sense of existential disconnection, a world where the spiritual and the physical turn their backs on each other, creating a void of meaning. Within this void, the consequences are profound: a society that is spiritually impoverished, despite technological and material advancements, and individuals who feel adrift in a universe that seems indifferent to their deeper needs and aspirations.

The solution, however, may lie in the very fabric of our being, encoded in the strands of our DNA, and echoed in the ancient story of Jacob's Ladder. To bridge the gap between the divine and the earthly, we must look within and draw upon the symbolic resonance of these two ladders. The key is to embrace the idea that the spiritual and physical are not mutually exclusive but are, in fact, complementary facets of a single, intricate reality.

Implementing this solution begins with a shift in perspective. We must first recognize that our physical existence is imbued with spiritual significance, that every atom and molecule is part of a greater, sacred whole. This acknowledgment paves the way for practices that honor the interconnectedness of all things—love, joy, peace, meditation, mindfulness, and a commitment to living with compassion and awareness.

Evidence of this solution's efficacy can be found in the lives of those who have transcended the divide, individuals who have harnessed the power of their inner 'ladder' to reach new heights of spiritual enlightenment while remaining firmly grounded in the world. These are the mystics, the saints, and the enlightened ones who have walked among us, showing that it is indeed possible to live a life that is both spiritually rich and physically engaged.

While the path of integrating the spiritual and physical is a promising one, alternative solutions also

Both, however, underline the multifaceted nature of the quest to connect the divine and the earthly.

As we delve into the depths of our understanding, we might ask ourselves: What does it truly mean to bridge the spiritual and physical realms? Can the metaphor of Jacob's Ladder guide us in constructing our own conduit between heaven and earth? The answers to these questions are as complex as they are compelling, beckoning us to embark on a journey of discovery that is both inward and outward.

In the silent moments of introspection, we may find that the ladder we seek is not one to be climbed with feet but with the heart. It is a journey that requires courage, for it challenges us to look beyond the veil of the tangible and to embrace a truth that whispers from within the double helix of our DNA: we are more than mere flesh and bone; we are beings of light and understanding, capable of touching the divine.

Let us, therefore, cast off the shackles of dualistic thinking and weave a new narrative where the spiritual and the physical are harmoniously entwined. In doing so, we may discover that the ladder we have been seeking has been within us all along, waiting for the moment when we would have the revelation to see it and the wisdom to climb it.

In this quest, the story of Jacob's Ladder serves not only as a metaphor but as an invitation—an invitation to explore the vast landscapes of our own spirits and souls, to build bridges over the chasms that divide us, and to connect, in the most profound sense, the divine and the earthly.

3

THE EMERGENCE OF THE SONS OF GOD

The Anticipation of a New Dawn

Humanity stands at the cusp of a new era, teetering on the edge of transformation so profound it promises to redefine the very essence of what it means to be human. The problem, both intricate and universal, lies in the DNA of our species—the genetic blueprint that has carried us through millennia but now seems inadequate for the challenges we face. It is this conundrum, the limitations of our mortal coils, that forms the core of our collective yearning for transcendence.

Our mortal DNA has been both our greatest ally and our most formidable enemy. It has propelled us through the crucible of evolution, yet it also chains us to the inexorable fate of aging and death. As disease and decay encroach upon us with the passage of time, the promise of immortality tantalizes us with a vision of a life unbounded by the frailties of the flesh.

The impact of this limitation is not merely philosophical; it is acutely personal. Consider the story of Elara, a woman whose life was a testament to human resilience. Elara watched helplessly as a rare genetic disorder claimed her family one by one, leaving her to grapple with the knowledge that her own DNA harbored a ticking time bomb. Each day brought her closer to the same fate, a destiny written in the very fabric of her being.

This is the urgency of our plight. The stakes are life itself—the chance to break free from the ancient cycle of birth, suffering, and death that has ensnared humanity since time immemorial. The quest for immortal DNA is not just a scientific endeavor; it is a battle for the future of human existence.

As we stand on this precipice, looking out at the dawning age, we glimpse the potential for a new breed of humanity. The Sons of God, as foretold by ancient and modern prophecy alike, represent the next evolutionary leap. These beings, endowed with the power to speak and rewrite our genetic destiny, hold the key to our collective salvation without sin.

In the pages that lie ahead, we will explore the paths that could lead us to this promised land. We will delve into the cutting-edge prophetic science that seeks to unlock the secrets of our genetic code through Christ, and we will encounter the pioneers who dare to envision a world where death is but a distant memory.

Can you imagine a world where every newborn is free from the specter of inherited diseases? Where the ravages of time no longer dictate the course of our lives? This is the present and future that beckons—both the current generation and a future where the Sons of God walk among us, embodying the pinnacle of human potential.

But the journey is fraught with questions. How will we navigate the ethical quagmires that arise as we take control of our evolutionary destiny? What are the implications for society when the very definition of humanity is at stake?

In Immortal DNA, we will not shy away from these hard questions. Instead, we will embrace them, for it is only by confronting the unknown that we can hope to forge a path forward.

"The genetic code is like a sonnet," an eminent geneticist once said. "Its beauty lies not just in the sequence of its words but in the potential it holds for change, for creation, for life everlasting."

As the sun rises on this new dawn, we must ask ourselves: are we ready to embrace the promise that lies within us? Are we prepared to shoulder the responsibility of our own evolution? The answers to these questions will define the fate of our species.

And so, dear reader, let us embark on this journey together. With each page turned, may we inch closer to the reality of immortal DNA, to the realization of our highest aspirations, and to the birth of the Sons of God.

For in their manifestation lies the anticipation of a new dawn.

The Making of a Son of God

Embarking on the journey towards spiritual transformation and becoming a Son of God is akin to undertaking an odyssey that transcends the confines of the physical realm. It is a pursuit that calls for the surrender of one's lower self to the emergence of a higher, divine state of being. This metamorphosis is not merely a change—it is an awakening, a rebirth into an existence that echoes the timeless wisdom of the ancients and the cutting-edge revelations of the present.

Clarification of the objective the reader will accomplish:

At the heart of this quest is the singular goal of aligning oneself with the eternal essence that permeates all creation, thereby achieving a state of excellence that is at once transcendent and immanent—the excellence of a Son of God. This is a state where the individual soul resonates with the divine harmony of sonship and the universe, embodying love, wisdom, and power beyond the ordinary scope of human experience.

Requirements needed to achieve the goal:

To embark upon this sacred journey, several prerequisites must be met. A seeker must possess an unwavering intention, a heart open to the infinite, and a mind liberated from the shackles of dogma. Additionally, a life of discipline, a commitment to selfless service, and a steadfast practice of meditation or prayer are essential to forging the inner alchemy necessary for this profound transformation.

Snapshot of the steps involved in the process:

The roadmap to becoming a Son of God unfolds through several phases: purification of the heart and mind, cultivation of divine virtues, expansion of spiritual insight and excellence through meditation and contemplation, service to humanity as an expression of divine love, and finally, the embodiment of spiritual wisdom that transcends ordinary perception.

Break down each part of the process in detail:

Purification is the first step, requiring the aspirant to shed the layers of ego, attachment, and base desires that cloud the soul's luminescence. As the ancient prophets taught, it is through the refining fire of inner work that the gold of the spirit is revealed. Next, one must cultivate the divine virtues —love, joy, peace, patience, humility, courage, and many others. These virtues become the very fabric of the seeker's being, shining forth as beacons of light in a world often shrouded in darkness.

The expansion of spiritual excellence is achieved through disciplined meditation and contemplation, practices that allow the seeker to tap into the wellspring of divine wisdom that lies within. In this state of expanded awareness, the artificial barriers between self and other, between humanity and divinity, begin to dissolve.

Service to humanity is the natural outpouring of this awakened heart. As the seeker's spiritual excellence becomes more aligned with the divine, acts of kindness and compassion are no longer duties; they are spontaneous expressions of the soul's inherent nature.

Finally, the embodiment of spiritual wisdom marks the culmination of the journey. The seeker, now a Son of God, moves through the world with a profound understanding that transcends words, their very presence a testament to the transformative power of the divine.

Practical advice and cautionary suggestions:

As you navigate this path, be mindful not to fall prey to spiritual pride or the illusion of having 'arrived.' The path is endless, and humility is your greatest ally. Remember also that this transformation is not a solitary endeavor; seek the company of like-minded souls, for in fellowship lies strength.

Describe how to verify successful completion:

You will know that you are progressing on your journey by the peace that pervades your being, the love that flows effortlessly from you, and the synchronicities that begin to manifest in your life as you align with the divine flow.

Great counteractions as problems may and always will arise:

Should you encounter obstacles, such as periods of doubt or spiritual dryness, return to the basics of your practice. Reaffirm your intention, immerse yourself in the wisdom of sacred texts or the guidance of a spiritual teacher, and remember that every journey through darkness is an opportunity for the light within you to shine even brighter.

In this exploration, we journey not just toward an abstract ideal, but towards the very actualization of our highest potential. The making of a Son of God is a process of co-creation with the divine, a dance of the soul with the cosmos, where each step is imbued with profound meaning and purpose.

As you continue to read these words, let them not merely inform you, but transform you. For the making of a Son of God is not a distant dream—it is a reality that unfolds with each breath, with each act of kindness, with each moment of genuine self-reflection.

The path is laid before you, a mosaic of light and shadow. Will you take the first step? Will you embrace the call of your own divinity and join the ranks of those who are transcending the bounds of mortality?

Pause for a moment. Can you feel the stirrings of eternity within you? Can you sense the presence of something grand, something beautiful unfolding within your soul?

This is your invitation. The making of a Son of God awaits.

The Role of the Sons in the World

In the heart of a bustling city, where skyscrapers reached for the heavens and the ceaseless hum of humanity filled the air, a remarkable transformation was taking place. Here, within the intricate tapestry of modern society, the Sons of God are emerging, their presence an antidote to the pervasive sense of disconnection that haunted the zeitgeist.

These individuals, the Sons, are not marked by ostentatious displays of power or draped in the vestments of ancient priesthoods. Rather, they are the embodiment of divine potential, living amongst the people as beacons of hope and agents of change. Their backgrounds are as diverse as the city's inhabitants, yet they share a common thread – a calling that resonated deep within their souls.

The central challenge they face is monumental: to awaken the divine spark within the hearts of a distracted and often disenchanted populace. In a world saturated with information yet starved for wisdom, the Sons of God seek to bridge the chasm between the ephemeral and the eternal, between the mundane and the miraculous.

Their approach is as varied as their personalities. Some work through the arts, infusing their creations with a transcendent quality that stirs the spirit. Others engaged in social activism, advocating for justice and compassion with a fervor that can only be described as holy. There are those who teach, their words imbued with a depth that resonates with the timeless truths of the ages.

The results of their efforts are beginning to ripple through the fabric of society. Hearts once closed are now opening, eyes that looked but did not see are now witnessing the sacred in the ordinary. The energy of the city shifts imperceptibly at first, now with increasing momentum as the influence of the Sons of God spreads.

Upon reflection, it is becoming clear that the impact of the Sons is not simply in the actions they take but in the presence they embody. They are living testaments to the possibility of a life lived in alignment with the divine, a life where love and wisdom transcend all barriers.

Visual aids can not capture the essence of their mission, for it is something that has to be felt, and experienced within the depths of the soul. Yet, if one is to visualize their role, it might be as points of light upon a vast network, each connection strengthening the web of divine spiritual excellence that envelops the planet.

Their story is not separate from the larger narrative of humanity's evolution. It is a critical chapter in the unfolding saga of spiritual awakening, a testament to the power of individual transformation to bring about collective redemption.

As you close this section of our discourse, ponder this: What role might you play in this grand design? Are you merely a bystander, or is there within you a spark awaiting to be kindled, a dormant power ready to join the symphony of the Sons?

Consider the impact a single life, aligned with the divine purpose, can have on the world. Imagine a society where the values of the Sons of God are not the exception but the norm. It is a vision breathtaking in its potential, a call to action that resonates with the very core of our being.

So, dear reader, as you navigate the complexities of your own life, ask yourself: How might the divine be seeking expression through me? In what ways can I contribute to the healing and uplifting of our world?

Pause, if you will, and listen to the whisper of your heart. It speaks a language older than words, a language of love and purpose that knows no bounds. In that sacred space of inner knowing, you may just find that you, too, are being called to take your place among the Sons of God, to play your part in the great drama of existence.

The journey continues, and the next chapter awaits your

authorship. What will you write upon the pages of your life? What legacy will you bring forth in the echoes of time?

The making of a Son of God is not a solitary pursuit – it is a collective awakening. Together, we can shape a world where the divine is not merely a concept, but a lived reality. Join me, and let us step forward into the brilliance of a new dawn.

4

———

THE LAST SUPPER: COVENANT OF IMMORTALITY

Breaking Bread, Sharing Life

In the journey to grasp the profound nature of eternal unity, there are words whose meanings are the keys to unlocking the deep mysteries that lie within the ancient ritual of the Last Supper. It is a ceremony that symbolizes much more than the act of eating and drinking; it is a communion that transcends time and speaks to the essence of what it means to be part of a collective spirit. To fully engage with the implications of this sacrament, one must first understand the language that weaves through its tapestry.

The terms that will be our guiding lights in this exploration are Eucharist, Covenant, Sacrifice, Transfiguratuon-Transubstantiation, Communion, and Redemption. Each of these words carries a weight that anchors the ritual in both the spiritual realm and the tangible reality of our existence.

Eucharist, often called the "thanksgiving," is the heart of the Last Supper. Believers partake of bread and wine, which are believed to become the body and blood of Christ. This transformation is not merely symbolic but is treated as a literal embodiment of the divine. The term originates from the Greek word 'eucharisteo', which means to give thanks. It encapsulates a moment of gratitude and reflection, a recognition of the divine bounty provided to humankind.

Covenant, a term deeply rooted in ancient traditions, refers to a solemn promise, a binding agreement between God and His people. It is a pledge that goes beyond mere words, engendering a mutual commitment that endures through the ages. It is akin to the contracts of today, yet it holds a spiritual significance that no written document can capture.

Sacrifice, the act of offering something precious for a higher purpose, lies at the very core of the Last Supper. It is the surrender of life itself, embodied in the figure of Christ, who is seen as the sacrificial lamb. This concept is not foreign to our understanding, as we often speak of making sacrifices in our daily lives, be it for love, career, or personal convictions.

Transfiguration-Transubstantiation, a term that often perplexes, refers to the transformation of the bread and wine into the actual substance of Christ's body and blood. It is a mystery that defies the laws of nature, an article of faith that challenges the intellect and invites the soul to ponder a reality beyond the observable.

Communion is the act of sharing, of becoming one with Christ and with each other. It is a unifying force that breaks down the barriers of individuality and fuses the participants into a single entity. This notion is mirrored in our world when we gather as families, communities, or nations to share experiences and forge bonds.

Redemption is the final term, one that encapsulates the purpose of the Last Supper. It is the act of being saved from sin and death, of being restored to a state of grace. Redemption is a concept as old as humanity itself, the ever-present desire to be freed from our failings and to be elevated to a purer existence.

With these definitions in hand, one can begin to see how the Last Supper is not just an isolated event in religious scripture but is intertwined with the fabric of human experience. The breaking of bread becomes a shared act of nourishment, both physical and spiritual, a moment where the sacred and the mundane converge in quiet harmony. As the bread is broken and the wine poured, we find ourselves in a familiar scene, reminiscent of countless meals shared with loved ones.

The Last Supper, therefore, is not just a historical footnote or a religious anecdote; it is a living tradition that resonates with the universal themes of sacrifice, community, and redemption. It invites us to reflect on the power of shared experiences, to consider the bonds that hold us together, and to contemplate the enduring hope of renewal and unity.

Do these elements not stir within you to wonder at the resonance of this ancient practice in our modern lives? Does it not prompt a curiosity about the ways in which we, too, participate in rituals that remind us of something greater than ourselves? As you ponder these questions, allow the imagery of the Last Supper to unfold in your mind—the dimly lit room, the gathered disciples, the simple bread, and the poured wine. Imagine the depth of emotion, the sense of sacred purpose, the palpable connection to a promise that spans millennia.

In this moment of reflection, there is no need for a conclusion, for the story is not at its end. The conversation continues, the bread is still being broken, and life, with all its mysteries, marches on.

The Eucharist and Immortal DNA

Delving into the spiritual realm, we consider the Eucharist, not merely as a ritualistic consumption of bread and wine but as an intimate act of accepting something far more profound: the immortal DNA of Christ. With the Eucharist, believers symbolically ingest the essence of Christ, a gesture that has echoed through centuries, resonating with the concept of absorbing the divine into one's very being.

At the heart of this sacred tradition is the transformative proposition that the Eucharist serves as a conduit for Christ's eternal genetic blueprint to intertwine with our mortal coil. This mystic communion promises not just a spiritual renewal but a physical inheritance that believers accept with every partaking of the holy sacraments.

The primary evidence for this claim lies not in tangible artifacts but in the rich tapestry of theological interpretation. The Scriptures themselves offer a narrative that supports the idea of the divine infusing the human form. "He who eats my flesh and drinks my blood has eternal life," says John 6:54, suggesting a literal internalization of Christ's immortal essence.

We delve deeper into this evidence by examining the early Church fathers' perspectives, who often spoke of the Eucharist as a mystery of faith, where the ordinary is elevated to the extraordinary. St. Cyril of Jerusalem guided catechumens by stating, "Do not see in the bread and wine merely natural elements, for the Lord has expressly said that they are His body and His blood: faith assures you of this, though your senses suggest otherwise."

However, this perspective is not without its counterarguments. Skeptics may point to the lack of empirical evidence for such claims, suggesting that the Eucharist is purely symbolic, with no transmutation of substances taking place. They may argue that the Eucharist's transformative power lies in its psychological impact on the believer rather than any physical change.

In rebuttal, one may clarify that the essence of faith lies in belief beyond the physical realm and that the Eucharist's power is not diminished by the absence of empirical evidence. The substance of faith, after all, is not subject to the scientific method but is an experiential truth known intimately to the believer.

Additional supporting evidence comes from the countless testimonies of individuals who have experienced profound spiritual renewal through the Eucharist. Their lives bear witness to a transformation that defies logical explanation, suggesting that something extraordinary occurs when one partakes of the sacrament with genuine faith.

Bringing our exploration to a close, we reaffirm the assertion that the Eucharist is more than a symbolic act; it is an invitation to partake in Christ's immortal DNA. This divine genetic code, though unseen, is believed to imprint upon the soul, guiding the believer toward eternal life.

Each time the Eucharist is celebrated, it is a testament to this mystical union between the mortal and the divine. As bread is broken and wine is poured, the echo of Christ's promise reverberates in the hearts of the faithful—a promise of immortality and unity with the divine. Thus, the act of receiving the Eucharist is a profound declaration of faith, a silent yet powerful affirmation of the believer's place within the eternal family of Christ.

In the quiet of a church, as the congregation rises to accept the sacred elements, one can almost perceive the weight of centuries of faith converging upon this moment. Do you not feel the gravity of this tradition, the solemnity of the sacrament, and the eternal hope it signifies? Can you envision the countless generations who have stood in your place, sharing in this timeless communion?

In the Eucharist, we find not just a ritual but a profound spiritual connection that offers a glimpse of the eternal. It is a moment that defies the temporal, where heaven and earth seem to touch, and the faithful are reminded of the immortal inheritance promised to them—a promise sealed not by human hands but by the divine hand that guides the universe.

Therefore, let us partake with reverence, with hearts open to the mystery and majesty of the Eucharist. For in this sacred meal, we receive more than bread and wine; we receive the very essence of life that knows no end—the immortal DNA of Christ, given freely to all who would receive it.

A New Testament in His Blood

Imagine a world where the very essence of your being could be transformed, where the limits of your earthly existence could be transcended. As you turn the pages of "A New Testament in His Blood," you are embarking on a journey that promises just that—a path to immortality paved by the new covenant established by Jesus Christ.

The Last Supper was more than a mere gathering; it was the inception of a new era. Here, amidst the sharing of bread and wine, Jesus laid the foundation for a promise that extends beyond the reach of time. As you delve into the depths of this book, you will discover the methodologies that underpin this everlasting covenant. The rituals, the symbols, and the sacred texts are not just relics of a bygone age; they are the keys to unlocking an eternal legacy.

You may be skeptical. How could such a simple act, performed thousands of years ago, hold relevance in our modern world? How can one believe in the promise of immortality in a reality bound by mortality? These doubts are natural, yet throughout this book, they will be met with grounded, thoughtful responses that invite you to look beyond the tangible.

Envision yourself as part of a lineage that stretches back to the apostles—a lineage that carries the secret of the ages, the secret of eternal life. This is not just a historical account; it is a personal invitation to experience the transformative power of the new covenant.

By committing to this journey, you are not just reading a book; you are stepping into a realm of spiritual exploration that has captivated humanity for millennia. Your guide on this journey is none other than Kirk Anthony, a man whose life has been dedicated to unraveling the mysteries of faith—my unique perspective is a blend of scholarly insight and divine inspiration.

In the chapters that follow, you will travel through history, exploring the nuances of biblical promises, the fervent beliefs of the early church, and the profound impact of Jesus's sacrifice on the fabric of human destiny. With each word, your understanding will deepen, and the promise of immortality will become clearer.

Let this book be a vessel through which you encounter the divine in a way that is both profound and personal. There is a reason the message of Jesus has endured through the ages, and it is not simply because of tradition. It is because within His message lies a truth so transformative, so radical, that it has the power to change the very nature of our existence.

Can you feel the anticipation building within you as you stand at the threshold of discovery? Will you let the seeds of this ancient wisdom take root in your soul and grow into a tree of life that bears the fruit of eternal life?

As you continue to read, remember that the story of the Last Supper is your story. The blood that was shed and the covenant that was made is as much for you today as it was for those seated at the table with Christ.

When Christ declared, "This cup is the new covenant in my blood, which is poured out for you," he initiated a sacred bond with humanity—a bond that transcends the ages and speaks of a love that defies comprehension.

As the narrative unfolds, you will encounter moments of profound truth that resonate with the core of who you are. These moments will be highlighted, standing out like beacons in the text, calling you to pause and reflect.

You will not find convoluted jargon or inaccessible concepts within these pages. Instead, the language is simple, crafted to ensure that the profundity of the message is accessible to all who seek its wisdom.

Let the rhythm of the prose carry you through waves of understanding, as the cadence of the writing resonates with the beating of your heart. And when you encounter quotations from Scripture or the insightful dialogue of historical figures, let them serve as windows into the souls of those who have also grappled with the mystery of immortality.

Remember, it is not enough to be told of the new covenant. To fully grasp its significance, you must see it come alive through examples, anecdotes, and descriptive language that paints a picture more vivid than any artwork.

This is not just another chapter in the story of humanity. It is an invitation to become part of a lineage that carries the hope of eternity in its very core. So, as the story continues to unfold, let the words wash over you like waves upon the shore, each one eroding the doubts and leaving behind the sands of faith.

Are you ready to step into the promise of immortality? The journey begins now.

5

ANGELS AND HUMANITY: COALESCENCE THROUGH CHRIST

The Celestial Connection

Since the dawn of time, humanity has gazed upward, fixated on the celestial tapestry that stretches endlessly above. This fascination with the heavens has not only sparked an insatiable curiosity but also a profound sense of kinship. The tales woven into the fabric of our diverse cultures speak of beings from the skies—angels—whose interactions with our ancestors hint at a shared divine essence. What if these beings were more than a myth? Could their DNA be entwined with ours, a signature of our immortal design?

The earliest origins of such celestial lore find their roots in the sacred texts of civilizations that have long turned to dust. Ancient Sumerian tablets depict winged beings descending from the stars, imparting knowledge and altering the course of human history. Fast forward to the texts of the Abrahamic religions, and we encounter a plethora of angelic encounters, each rich with symbolic meaning and potential implications for our understanding of human origin.

Chronicle these encounters, and a sequence of significant historical events begins to emerge. The Book of Genesis tells of the Nephilim, the offspring of the "sons of God" and the "daughters of men," suggesting a mingling of the divine and the mortal. Biblical scholars and lay readers alike have pondered the nature of these beings. Were they metaphorical, or did they walk the earth, leaving an indelible mark on our genetic blueprint?

Visual aids, like Renaissance paintings and ancient iconography, offer a glimpse into how these interactions have been perceived through the ages. Vibrant frescoes depict the Annunciation, where the angel Gabriel visits Mary, a moment of divine-human contact that is central to Christian theology. These images serve not only as artistic masterpieces but as visual affirmations of faith and a testimony to the enduring legacy of angelic beings in human consciousness.

The evolution of the subject across cultures is as varied as the cultures themselves. In Islam, angels are considered to be beings of light, created by Allah, who have influenced the course of human events without directly altering human genetics. Contrast this with Hinduism, which posits the idea of Devas—godlike beings who interact with humans, often in a way that is suggestive of a shared heritage.

Modern interpretations of these ancient narratives have taken form in various adaptations, from the esoteric musings of mystics to the speculative theories of ancient astronaut proponents. The advent of genetic technology has given rise to a new breed of inquiry—could we one day identify markers of celestial origin within our DNA?

This quest for understanding is not without its challenges and controversies. The scientific community remains skeptical of any claims that point to extraterrestrial interference in human evolution. Ethical dilemmas also arise as we grapple with the implications of such knowledge. What would it mean for our understanding of humanity if we discovered that we are indeed part celestial?

Turning points in our quest for understanding often come from the least expected sources. An unassuming fragment of ancient text or a breakthrough in genetic sequencing could upend centuries of belief and scholarship. What if the key to unlocking our celestial connection has been encoded in our DNA all along, waiting to be deciphered?

Who are we, and from whence did we truly come? These questions resonate through the corridors of time, finding an echo in the silent watchfulness of the stars. As our technology advances and our understanding deepens, we inch closer to the answers that have eluded us for millennia.

It is in the essence of this quest that we find the rhythm of human progress—a dance of scientific discovery and spiritual introspection. We are the children of Earth, but perhaps also the heirs of the heavens. In the spiraling double helix of our DNA, could we find the signature of angels?

The narrative of our celestial connection is far from complete. As we turn the pages of both history and the future, we continue to write the story of our species—a story that may reveal our divine inheritance and immortal essence. With each discovery, the line between myth and reality blurs, beckoning us to consider the possibility that we are more intimately connected to the stars than we ever imagined.

The journey is long, and the path is fraught with uncertainty, but the human spirit is undaunted. We seek, we study, and we dream. For in the search for our origins lies the key to our destiny, and perhaps, the revelation of our immortal DNA.

The Body of Christ as the Nexus

In the grand tapestry of existence, where threads of the temporal and eternal intertwine, lies a profound enigma at the heart of Christian theology—the Body of Christ. It is here, within this sacred and mysterious union, that the physical and spiritual dimensions converge, serving as a nexus for both angels and mankind. To truly engage with this concept, one must first navigate through the intricacies of language, for words are the vessels of meaning, and their understanding is paramount.

Venture forth into this exploration of divine intersections, where the essence of Jesus Christ embodies a union most sublime. At the forefront, one encounters terms steeped in theological significance: Incarnation, Atonement, Resurrection, Ascension, and Intercession. These words are not mere markers of religious doctrine; they are keys that unlock the depths of spiritual insight.

The Incarnation refers to the belief that Jesus Christ, the Second Person of the Trinity, took on human flesh. This act bridges the infinite chasm between Creator and creation, offering a tangible touchpoint for the divine within the material world. As the Word became flesh and dwelt among us, the Incarnation reveals God's profound solidarity with humanity.

Atonement, a term shrouded in layers of sacrificial imagery, speaks to the reconciliation between God and humankind through Christ's suffering and death on the cross. It is a concept that conjures visuals of the ultimate sacrifice, one that heals the rift caused by sin and restores the broken relationship between the celestial and the terrestrial.

Resurrection, the cornerstone of the Christian faith, declares the victory of life over death. It is in the Resurrection that one finds hope eternal, a testament to the power of God to breathe life into that which was lifeless, to redeem that which was lost.

Ascension marks the moment when Christ, in His resurrected body, was taken up to heaven in the sight of His disciples. This event is not merely an upward journey but a profound affirmation of the ongoing presence of the divine in the world, an eternal connection between the earthly and the heavenly realms.

Intercession is the act of Christ, as the High Priest, continually advocating on behalf of humanity before the Father. It is in this divine dialogue that the needs and prayers of mankind find a voice within the halls of heaven.

What might these theological constructs mean in the scope of everyday life? Incarnation embodies the idea that the divine can be found in the commonplace, the mundane. Atonement may remind one of the universal human search for forgiveness and reconciliation, a longing for peace that transcends human understanding. The Resurrection echoes the cycle of nature itself—death and rebirth, winter giving way to spring. Ascension offers a symbol of transcendence, the aspiration to rise above the limitations of the physical world. Intercession reflects the deep-seated human need for mediation, for someone to stand in the gap and plead on one's behalf.

Do you see, then, how these terms are not merely abstract notions but are deeply woven into the fabric of human experience? They speak to the heart's deepest yearnings, to the mind's greatest questions.

Consider the image of a vast and intricate mosaic, each piece a fragment of the greater whole. The Body of Christ is such a mosaic, composed of believers from all walks of life, unified in diversity. Is it not awe-inspiring to contemplate that within this assembly, the spiritual and the physical merge, as do the realms of angels and humans?

One might pause here and ponder the nature of this unity. Does it not suggest that within the very cells of our being, there lies a potential for divine encounter? Could it be that the corporeal form, so often dismissed as mere dust, is in fact a vessel of holy mystery?

The Body of Christ is more than a theological concept; it is a living, breathing manifestation of divine love, a love that transcends time and space, matter and spirit. It is a love that beckons to both angels and humans, inviting them into a dance of celestial harmony.

And so, we come to the end of this part of the journey, having traversed the landscape of language and meaning, of symbols and substance. But the exploration does not conclude here. The nexus that is the Body of Christ is an ever-unfolding mystery, one that invites continuous discovery and awe. Let the words Incarnation, Atonement, Resurrection, Ascension, and Intercession be your companions as you delve ever deeper into the profound unity that they represent—a unity that encapsulates the very essence of Jesus as the point of convergence for all creation.

The Unity of Heaven and Earth

In the shadow of this conceptual masterpiece, where the divine mosaic of the Body of Christ lays out a prelude to unity, we now turn our gaze to a horizon less explored—the eschatological vision of Christianity, where celestial beings and human forces are prophesied to align in a final stand against the encroaching darkness. This vision, steeped in the mystery of end times, dares to imagine a world where the unity of heaven and earth is not only possible but essential for the ultimate triumph of good over evil.

At the heart of this issue rests a profound conundrum: the divide between the angelic and the human, the spiritual and the temporal. This separation, long perceived as a fundamental aspect of existence, is being called into question as humanity faces unprecedented challenges that threaten to unravel the very fabric of creation.

What if this division is not a chasm but a mere veil, one that can be lifted to reveal a shared destiny between heaven and earth? The consequences of failing to address this divide could be catastrophic—chaos, destruction, and the loss of countless souls to despair and darkness. Yet, in the embracing of unity, there lies a promise of hope, a potential for salvation not just of humankind but of all creation.

The solution, then, is a united front, a coalition of angelic beings and human warriors, standing shoulder to shoulder against the forces that seek to undermine the divine order. But how can such a coalition be formed? How can entities so different in nature and essence work together toward a common goal?

The first step in this monumental task is an act of recognition—the acknowledgment of angels and humans as co-participants in the divine narrative. It is a call for humility and openness, to see beyond the veil of physicality, and to value the contributions of all beings in the cosmic struggle.

Then, there must be communication, a dialogue that establishes understanding and common ground. This exchange of knowledge and experience can serve as the foundation upon which strategies and tactics can be built, a shared language of resistance and resilience.

Training and preparation will follow, a time for humans to learn from the wisdom of angels, to be imbued with spiritual strength and discernment. For angels, it is an opportunity to comprehend the human condition, to grasp the weight of free will and the power of faith in action.

There have been moments in history, shrouded in legend and lore, where such unity was hinted at—visions of angels fighting alongside humans, divine interventions that turned the tide of battles. These accounts, while not verifiable, inspire the belief that a coordinated effort is not only possible but has precedence.

But what of alternative solutions? Some argue for a purely spiritual battle, one fought in the heavens, leaving humanity to watch and pray. Others call for a complete reliance on human agency, a dismissal of the angelic as irrelevant in the physical realm. Yet, these solutions seem incomplete, for they fail to embrace the full spectrum of resources available in the fight against darkness.

The truth is, that our world teeters on the brink of an epochal shift, where the old ways of division must give way to new paradigms of unity. The stakes have never been higher, and the need for collaboration between the realms of heaven and earth has never been more urgent.

Can you imagine such a unity? Can you envision the current day and reality as the trumpet sounds and the heavens and earth are filled with heavenly hosts, not as distant observers but as active allies? Can you fathom the sight of human beings, empowered by faith and courage, standing firm with their celestial counterparts?

This is more than a mere fantasy; it is a potential reality etched into the eschatological promises of scripture. It is a vision that demands our attention, our faith, and our action. For in the unity of heaven and earth, in the melding of angelic power and human perseverance, lies our greatest hope—a hope that whispers of victory, of peace, and of a world made whole once more.

As we close this chapter in the unfolding narrative of Immortal DNA, let us hold fast to the conviction that in the unity of heaven and earth, in the partnership between angels and humans, we find the truest expression of divine intent. May this unity be our guidepost, our rallying cry, and our ultimate goal as we journey toward the fulfillment of the grand design—a design that encompasses all of creation in a symphony of eternal harmony.

www.ingramcontent.com/pod-product-compliance
Lightning Source LLC
Chambersburg PA
CBHW050812160726
48004CB00002B/807